The
Secret
of Wealth

The Secret of Wealth

Owen Phelps, Ph.D.

TDC

The Durand Corporation

Durand, Illinois 61024

The Secret of Weatlh

For more information about this book, or the topics of wealth, abundance and philanthropy, or about its author visit the World Wide Web site:

http://www.SOWAbundance.net

The author is CEO of the Midwest Leadership Institute (MLI). For more information about MLI, visit its World Wide Web site:

http://www.MidwestLeadershipInstitute.net

Library of Congress Control Number: 2006910842

ISBN-13: 978-0-9769210-1-1
ISBN-10: 0-9769210-1-4

Publisher's Cataloging-in-Publication
(Provided by Quality Books, Inc.)

Phelps, Owen.
   The secret of wealth / by Owen Phelps.
   p. cm.
   LCCN 2006910842
   ISBN-13: 978-0-9769210-1-1
   ISBN-10: 0-9769210-1-4

   1. Success—Psychological aspects. 2. Well-being.
   3. Wealth. 4. Generosity.   I. Title.

BF637.S8P44 2007   158.1
                          QBI06-600711

Printed in the United States of America.

Dedication

To my parents, Joan and Owen, whose lives always modeled abundance, most especially in times of scarcity ... to Jane, whose generous gift of herself has made my life unspeakably abundant ... to our children, their spouses, and our grandchildren, and to our siblings and their families — all of whom remind me each day of the Secret's incredible power.

Table of Contents

Introduction

On the cover of this book, you read that I am America's wealthiest man. It's true.

Of course, I'm not America's richest man.

You may be wondering, "What's the difference?"

Answering that question is the purpose of this book.

But let me say this much at the start. As words are used in this book, rich refers to an absolute measure of capital assets. So there can only be one "richest man" or "richest person" in any group. The one with the most assets wins the title.

Wealth is very different. It refers to the abundance that one experiences in life.

Rich measures something which exists outside of you. Wealth measures something that grows up deep inside of you and makes your life qualitatively different — in fact, much better.

Many people seek to become rich so that they can have the experience of being wealthy. They want the sense of well-being that abundance provides. Unfortunately, the world is full of people who have large incomes, even great riches in the form of assets, and yet they have not found the wealth — genuine abundance — which is the real point of their quest.

Here is what one of them said after he had started with nothing, became a millionaire by age 28 and built a fortune so large that he could afford to give the Smithsonian its largest gift ever —$100 million: "I believed that money would bring happiness. And I believed that I had acquired everything my quest for more could provide. Still, I had not found joy."[1]

Eventually this man did find joy — true wealth and a sense of deep abundance — pursuing the goal of giving away a wheelchair to every one of the 150 million people in the world today who need them. He has not achieved his goal — yet.

But his goal has given his life new purpose.

Once he was rich and enjoyed all the things money could buy. Today he enjoys the sense of purpose and peace of mind that no amount of money by itself can obtain. Today he knows the joy of being truly wealthy.

In the same way, America's two richest men — Bill Gates and Warren Buffet — have made headlines in recent years not because they have accumulated more riches but because they have decided to give away most of their vast fortunes. Apparently being the richest people in America is not enough. Now they want to be wealthy too.

The good news is that one does not have to first become a billionaire or even a millionaire in order to be wealthy. Just as the world is full of people who are rich but know nothing of the joy that comes from being wealthy, the world also is bursting with people who are not materially rich and yet know the joy of living truly wealthy lives.

They have discovered the Secret of Wealth.

The purpose of this book is to share that secret with you so that you can unlock the power of wealth in your life and know the priceless joy of abundance which is given only to the world's wealthiest people.

There can be only one "richest man" or "richest person" at any one time and place. But the title of "wealthiest" can be shared. In fact, it is meant to be held in common. Why? Because as your sense of wealth grows, the world we share is enriched.

Now I urge you — break open the secret. Embrace the secret. Embody the secret. And feast on the wealth that is waiting for you.

[1] The story of Ken Behring is told in AARP magazine (September-October, 2004).

4

1. The Twins

Olivia and Todd were curious 12-year-old twins who had the incredible fortune of living just a few blocks from a wonderful bookstore where they had come to know Mr. Peabody.

Mr. Peabody worked part-time at the bookstore, but he seemed to live there almost full-time. If he was roaming the aisles wearing a vest with the store's name discreetly printed over the left breast pocket, he was working. If he was sitting in a booth at the coffee bar with a book on the table in front of him, he was just there.

The twins had met Mr. Peabody by accident one day when they went to the bookstore to buy their mother a gift for her birthday. It was a late Saturday afternoon and most of the stores in town would be closing in a half hour. They had put off the task and then forgotten it for a few days. In truth, they went to the bookstore because time was scarce and it was the closest place to buy anything. They had no idea what to their buy their mother, but they knew she liked to read and they figured in a store full of books they could find something she might like.

After a few moments in the store they were full of doubt. Surrounded by various displays of books about a host of topics, they were overwhelmed. They realized they could not tell how a book would appeal to their mother by its cover — and yet they really had no other basis on which to make a choice.

That's when they met Mr. Peabody.

He had quietly slipped up on them, so the simple question he asked startled both of them. "Can I help you?"

They turned to find a short, round, slightly stooped old man with just a wisp of hair on the top of his head. His eyes twinkled and his smile was the sort that could melt the hardest heart — or put startled adolescent twins instantly at ease.

"We have a problem," said Olivia.

"And what is that?" the old man asked. His voice was as warm as his smile was wide, making it clear that his interest was genuine.

Olivia rattled off all the things that had brought them to this seemingly impossible situation. As she spoke, her sense of helplessness and guilt grew. Todd nodded in agreement every time Olivia took a breath.

When she finished he waited just a fraction of a moment, as if to allow Olivia's free floating anxiety a chance to settle on the floor. Then, through his smile, he said ever so softly, "I think we have just the thing for your mother. Follow me."

In a few seconds he was standing in front of a small shelf of small books, one of which he pulled out and handed to Olivia.

Olivia opened the book to find a brief and simple tale of children who dearly loved their mother. From page to page they struggled to tell her why and how they loved her in more than a dozen different ways. Olivia was touched by how so many of the little accounts paralleled her own experiences and feelings.

She didn't notice that Todd was looking over her shoulder until she heard him say, "Olivia, that could be us. It's perfect!" They looked up when they heard the old man's soft voice ask, "What do you think?" Todd was about to repeat his judgment that the book would make a perfect gift when Olivia, always the more practical, asked: "How much?"

"It's nine dollars," said the old man without bothering to look at the book's cover for a price. "Nine dollars and a few cents for tax," he corrected himself.

"That's all?" asked Todd, grabbing the book from Olivia's grasp and handing it over to Mr. Peabody. "We'll take it."

So began the precious friendship of the 12-year-old twins and Mr. Peabody, the retired school teacher who was recently widowed and, at this moment, just happened to have some room in his heart and some time on his hands to share with two young children the wonders of the universe — and their important places in it.

8

2. A Learning Opportunity

Before long Olivia and Todd were drifting down to the bookstore at every chance — and even inventing some opportunities to drop in on the kindly and wise old man. They were pleased to nearly always find Mr. Peabody there, although sometimes they found him working in the aisles.

If they would find him before or after his shifts he would be sitting in a booth with a book before him, his head bent over its pages, his reading glasses hanging precariously from the end of his oversize nose. Always they would slide into the booth across the table from him and ask the same question. "What are you doing, Mr. Peabody?"

He always had an answer. And it never was, "I'm reading a book" — even though that was always clearly the case. Once he told them, "I'm touring Africa," and then turned his book to reveal the cover of a collection of photographs of that vast place.

Before long the twins noticed a few unusual things about Mr. Peabody that they discussed on their way home from the bookstore. For one thing, he eventually seemed to know the answer to every question they had. For another, he often answered their questions not with answers but with questions of his own. Sometimes it was fun answering Mr. Peabody's "questions-back," as the twins called them. Sometimes it was a struggle.

But over the months of that marvelous summer, they learned that Mr. Peabody's questions always got them to a Big Answer. That's what they called it. And sometimes

— in a most amazing way that they could never quite explain — when they eventually got to the Big Answer it felt as if they had already known it. That made them feel good about themselves and their ability to figure things out on their own.

There was one more thing about Mr. Peabody.

He always had time for them. Even when he was working, he was never rushed and he was always glad to see them. They noticed that he always wore a smile, but when he saw them his smile always grew larger. So if they came into the bookstore to visit him and they didn't find him in a booth, they strolled around the store until they found him and caught his attention. If he was with a customer, they'd wave and keep on moving. But if he was alone they approached him and asked, "When are you getting off work today, Mr. Peabody?"

3. Growing Curiosity

At 12 years of age Olivia and Todd were just starting to put aside the things of childhood. It wasn't a sad process. In fact, the endearing but silly aspirations of childhood weren't slipping away as much as they were being crowded out by a whole new set of hopes, dreams, schemes and wonders. All of these seemed to be things that are unique to 12-year-olds — and to the rest of us who never lose the urge to wonder.

Olivia no longer aspired to be a princess — although she still thought it would be nice to live in a palace and enjoy the privilege of getting everything her heart could desire. Perhaps some day, she had been dreaming lately, she would be rich. Maybe it would officially occur when she was promoted from vice president to CEO of a major company — like a woman she had read about and admired instantly, although the details had long since gotten too fuzzy to recall.

Todd no longer boasted that he planned to be a doctor-fireman-bulldozer driver, and he was embarrassed when his mother brought it up. He now thought he might want to be a lawyer. His association with Mr. Peabody had him thinking lately about possibly becoming a teacher but he was bothered by what he'd heard about teachers not making much money. He did not want to be a teacher if he wasn't going to make much money because he was pretty sure people who were always short of money could not be happy.

As the days passed and Olivia and Todd talked about the kind of lives they would like to lead someday when they grew up, they found themselves talking more and more about money — the things it could buy, why they couldn't buy everything they wanted, and what they could do to have more money to buy more things. They had begun to notice the differences in people's lifestyles and realized that some people were rich and others were poor. Some, it seemed, could have everything they wanted while others had almost nothing.

In their own lives they agreed that getting things made them happy, so they were pretty sure that rich people were happier than poor people. It seemed that way in school too, where some kids always had new clothes and shoes and backpacks — and everything looked just like the things in TV and magazine ads, right down to the right brand names. The rich kids took trips to places the twins knew about only from watching television. The twins envied that and agreed that if their family was richer they would be happier.

But on occasion they wondered why some of the rich kids at school didn't seem very happy at all. They also wondered why many of the celebrities they heard about and read about were so unhappy. They had millions, even gadzillions of dollars so they could do whatever they wanted to do. But instead of enjoying life without limits, some of these celebrities made themselves miserable and destroyed their lives with drugs and alcohol. Some even killed themselves. None of this made any sense to the twins.

The more they thought and talked about all these things, the more confused they felt. One day Olivia suggested that they should ask Mr. Peabody about it. Todd objected. "What does he know about being rich?" Todd asked. "He was a school teacher who's still working part-time. I'll bet he doesn't know anything about being rich."

But Olivia liked her idea. "Mr. Peabody always knows the answer to every question we ever ask him," she declared. "And besides, you don't know for sure that he's not rich. Maybe he inherited money or won the lottery or just saved a lot. You don't know. And even if he is poor, he won't get mad. He's our friend. And he likes us asking questions. He told us so, and I believe him." She took a breath. "Todd, if we don't ask him we might never know how to be rich — and then we will hate our poor selves for the rest of our lives."

Olivia was always being melodramatic, so Todd was not impressed with her assessment of the risk. But he had to admit that everything else she said made perfect sense. So he agreed that the next time they saw Mr. Peabody, they would ask him if he knew the secret of wealth — and if he did, if he would be willing to share it.

14

4. Getting Rich

The very next afternoon, after they had finished their chores and their lunch, their mother agreed that they could head down to the bookstore. She asked the children what they would like for dinner, and added: "I don't know what's attracting you to that bookstore all the time, but I can think of worse places for you to hangout. And I sure love the birthday gifts you found for me there — especially that book. So have a good time and be back for dinner by 5."

The twins were out the door in a wink.

At the bookstore they found Mr. Peabody sitting in his favorite booth, bent over a book, his reading glasses again hanging precariously from his oversize nose. "What are you doing, Mr. Peabody?" they asked, ready for his always different, often amazing answer.

"I'm getting rich," he replied.

Todd and Olivia looked at each other in wonder. "That's exactly what we were going to ask you about, Mr. Peabody. Can you tell us how to become rich?" Olivia asked.

"I can do better than that," Mr. Peabody said. "I can tell you how to become wealthy."

Olivia and Todd looked at each other again, but this time in confusion. They weren't sure what he meant. How were "becoming rich" and "becoming wealthy" different? But whatever he meant, the offer sounded irresistible. They scrambled into the booth facing the old man as Todd spoke, "Go for it, Mr. Peabody. We've been wondering about this for a long, long time."

16

5. The Question

"It all begins with a question," said Mr. Peabody. "As you probably know by now, most everything begins with either a story or a question. The Secret of Wealth begins with a question. It's a complicated secret, so pretty soon it requires a story. But let's start with a question. Why do you want to know the Secret of Wealth?"

The twins were challenged by the question. Each sat still, hoping that the other would go first. Finally, Olivia took the lead.

"Okay, I want to be rich—or wealthy, if there's a difference—because I want to have a nice life. I think having a nice life means having nice things, and nice friends, of course. But nice things are important too. In fact, I'm not sure if you can have nice friends unless you have some nice things. They seem to go together. Also, I want to be comfortable. I don't want to worry. And I want people to like me. That's about it," she said, but she couldn't resist a succinct summary. "Like I want to have friends, have fun and feel good about myself."

Todd had formulated his answer by now. "I just want to be sort of rich — or wealthy, as you say. I mean, I don't want to be rich like a rock star, with millions and zillions of dollars to mess up my life. But I want to have some stuff. You know, an apartment with a big TV to watch games. And a car, a sports car. And maybe a truck or an SUV for camping and hunting. I want to look sharp at work so people respect me, and I want to look sharp when I'm out with the guys so I get a girlfriend."

"You want a girlfriend?" an astounded Olivia interrupted.

"Not now I don't!" Todd snapped.

Todd turned back to the old man and continued. "I don't want to be a rich snob or anything like that, you know? I just want to have some stuff. And later, when I get married — or I mean, if I get married — I want to have a nice house for my family and a van to go places. Of course, I'll have to pay for my children's education and stuff like that. That's how and why I want to be rich. I want to do stuff and have fun."

Mr. Peabody's smile didn't change. "That all sounds pretty normal to me," he said. "So what are you worried about?"

"Worried?" echoed Todd, not quite sure what Mr. Peabody meant.

"Do you mean why do we think about being rich? Why do we wonder about it?" asked Olivia, also not sure what Mr. Peabody was asking.

"Perhaps that's a better way to put it," Mr. Peabody replied. "I was asking you why you are concerned about being rich."

Olivia always started talking right away, even when she didn't necessarily have something to say. "I'm not sure, Mr. Peabody. Doesn't everybody wonder about being rich?"

Mr. Peabody chuckled. "Maybe not everybody, Olivia. But I suppose most people in our culture are concerned about it, and many of them worry about it. Why do you think that is?"

Todd jumped in. "If you have nothing — no food, no clothes, no hope — like some of the kids we see on TV who live in other countries, maybe you don't even think about being rich. Maybe you don't even know the word. I think we wonder about it because it's all around us, all the time. It's like you can either be rich or you can be poor, and I think we all would rather be rich, you know?

"I do know," Mr. Peabody smiled.

"I think Todd's right," Olivia said. "If you grow up in a place where you only know hunger and poverty and everybody else is in the same situation, you would have no idea about being rich so you wouldn't think about it. But for us it's right out there in front of us all the time — like it's teasing us. There's always much more to have than you've already got. And once you know about things, I think it's natural to want them, at least some of them. Don't you think, Mr. Peabody?"

"Yes, I do think it's pretty natural for us to want many of the things we see," said Mr. Peabody. "And I agree, there's a lot to see in our world today. So it's pretty natural for us to want a lot too. But let me ask you this. Are you saying that the more we see, the more we want?"

"Hmm," Olivia mused. "I wasn't saying that on purpose, but maybe I was implying it. I was just saying that the more that's available to us, the more we each want. I never thought about it in those words before."

The more
we see,
the more
we want.

6. Tale of Two Sisters

Olivia was clearly intrigued by her own discovery: "The more we see, the more we want."

Todd was uneasy. "It's a little scary to think about it that way," he said. "I mean, if it's true that the more stuff there is, the more stuff we are going to want, then we are always going to be falling behind. Think about it. New things are being invented all the time — say 100 things a day. And how many do we get? Not even one a day. So every day the gap between what we could have and what we do have is getting bigger. In a sense, we're getting poorer every day. That's a sad thought, isn't it?"

"Yes it is," Mr. Peabody nodded. "And you're right. Things get invented much more quickly than we can buy them, so the gap widens all the time. If we focus on the gap, we will always be falling further and further behind. If we want to be happy, it seems we are going to have to change our focus, don't you agree?"

Neither Todd nor Olivia was sure where Mr. Peabody was planning to go with his question, but they agreed with his conclusion. So they shook their heads and waited for him to continue.

"Enough questions for now," he said. "We've made a lot of progress, but now it's time for a story."

Olivia and Todd instinctively leaned back in the booth and made themselves comfortable.

Mr. Peabody began his story.

# # #

Once, very long ago and far away, there lived two sisters. They were twins like you. They grew up very close to one another. In fact, it never failed to amaze them how much they were alike. They had the same hopes and dreams, sometimes even the same thoughts. As they grew into adulthood, each began to think of having a husband, a home of her own and children.

One day, when they were together, filling in the details of their shared dreams, Myra, the one with brown hair, asked Millie, the one with black hair, "Do you think having husbands and different homes and children of our own will pull us apart?"

Millie gasped. It took her a second to catch her breath. "Oh Myra, I never thought of that!" she said. "Maybe it will. Maybe we shouldn't grow up."

Myra tried to reassure her. "We have no choice, Millie. Besides, I'm not worried for two reasons. First, we will be so busy and so happy we won't have time to miss each other when we're apart. And second, we can still see each other every day."

The argument reassured Millie, and the twins went back to filling in the details of their dreams.

As luck would have it, they soon met two brothers who were very close. The two couples courted, fell in love and shared a twin wedding. They found homes just a few blocks apart in their small village. In all respects it looked as if they would live very similar lives and see each other nearly every day. But then fortune intervened.

The business in which Myra's husband worked flourished. When its owner died, his family prevailed on Myra's husband to take over control — enticing him with an offer to own part of the business immediately and all of it in time. As they welcomed three healthy children into the world, their circumstances continually improved until they were, by all estimations, quite rich. They moved several times, each time to a new and bigger house, and each time further away from where Myra's sister lived.

Meanwhile, the business Millie's husband was in stagnated. The owner, terrified by poor prospects, clung closely to his diminishing treasure. He deprived his workers of anything more than the basics — and in that way he deprived himself of the contributions his workers might have made to the company's welfare.

Like Myra, Millie had three children, but one of them was not healthy, and the child's many special needs were a drain on the family's meager resources. They lived from payday to payday, and slowly they slipped into deep poverty.

# # #

"So there you have it. End of story," said Mr. Peabody. "Myra and her husband were rich and Millie and her husband were poor."

Todd objected. "That's not a good story!"

"Why not?" Mr. Peabody asked. "I certainly had your attention."

"That's because we expected more," said Olivia. "We expected to learn a secret — the Secret of Wealth. Your story didn't teach us anything."

"That's because it's not over," Mr. Peabody smiled. "I take it you want me to continue?" The twins nodded and Mr. Peabody continued.

# # #

"What wasn't apparent to people who knew Myra and Millie and their husbands was what was happening in their hearts," said Mr. Peabody. "That's where the secret lived. Secrets are always to be found in the heart. So our story moves to their hearts and what was happening to the inner lives the sisters were living."

Because Myra could afford to hire people to help her care for her household, she spent a large part of each day going to the market by herself. There she saw many things to buy — even more than her bounty could provide on any given day. She also met other people in similar circumstances who came to the market with ample money to spend.

Often their encounters began when one of them was admiring something new and precious in the market, like a hand-crafted figurine or furniture pieces brought from foreign lands. A new piece would stop one of the shoppers in his or her tracks. Then another would notice the piece, and another, until other shoppers would notice the throng and join the group out of curiosity. Eventually, some of them would say how they needed it, and pretty soon someone would buy the piece. As a rule, the merchant had more, but in a few days he would be sold out and it would take him many more days, even weeks, to replenish his supply.

Soon the group that gathered in awe of a new thing would be split into several subgroups. There were those who bought an item right away while it was the object of everyone's interest. There were those who didn't buy at first, and then had to wait to get one when the supply was replenished. There also were some who waited until obsession for the new item subsided and the merchant put his remaining stock on sale. Finally, there were those who for some reason or another did not get the item.

In time it came to matter very much to Myra that she be in the first group. She bought many things and felt good about the place it seemed to give her in the social order.

Each time she made a purchase she could not wait to show it to her dear sister. And each time Millie would admire it. But always Millie asked a little question: "Does this thing make you happy?" Always Myra would respond, "Oh Millie, it thrills me. I think it's so nice. Don't you just love it?"

And always Millie would answer, "It is nice, Myra. And I can see that you love it."

Some things went unsaid.

Myra never answered Millie's question about whether or not the purchase made her happy because, in truth, while acquiring new things excited her and even gave her a sense of accomplishment, it did not quite make her happy.

And Millie never answered Myra's question about whether she loved the new object because she could not bring herself to love things.

7. Rich Sister?

As the years passed, Myra acquired more and more nice things. But she did not keep up with the market. As the city grew and prospered so did the market. Eventually it spread across vast acres. There were new things for Myra to see there every day. She tried to choose only the most important, judging on the basis of where crowds formed to admire new things. But the market was too big for her to completely tour every day.

Eventually it grew so large that there were vast parts of it that Myra never had time to get to. She focused on visiting the part where the very best things and the richest people could be found and tried not to think about the other parts of it.

As her family's income grew, so did their storehouse of possessions. Soon the family outgrew their home again and moved to a larger, more elaborate one. It was further from Millie's home, so the sisters came to see each other less often. Myra regretted that but she told herself it was unavoidable.

A bystander would have thought that Myra's happiness would grow with her family's income and possessions, but it did not happen quite that way.

Instead, Myra noticed that the family in the house next door had some things from the market she did not have. She noticed that the family in the house on the other side of her own had new furniture that was much nicer than her own. She noticed that a family which lived across the street had a larger home with more ornamental features.

She began to make lists of the things she needed so

that her family's circumstances would be at least equal in all ways with each and every family in her neighborhood. Week after week the list grew and grew until she found it a painful chore to read it from beginning to end.

As the list grew, her focus began to change. She noticed the many good things she had less and less. Instead, she noticed the things that others had and she lacked. Some days that was all she thought about. As time passed she became more reluctant to invite her neighbors to visit because the conviction grew in her heart that she and her home were not worthy and she would be mocked if her neighbors saw how little her family had.

At night she would retire and reflect on how much she lacked. There were coats she did not own. The market featured fine furniture she did not have. The streets were full of carriages more grand than hers. People went to places she had never seen. As the nights passed, her mood darkened and her sleep became more fitful. She wondered if the day would ever come when she would have the things she wanted, things that her friends would admire, things she could enjoy. As she lay in bed wondering and worrying night after night, she began to feel great sorrow for the things she didn't have — and for herself.

In time life grew mostly into a big burden and Myra took pleasure from almost nothing. There was just too much lacking in her life to feel any kind of joy.

As she lay in bed, she lifted a thought to the heavens: "There is so much I do not have. Please help me obtain more of it so that I might be happy."

8. Poor Sister?

Meanwhile, Millie's material circumstances became more dire by the day. One day, as Christmas drew near, her husband came home to report that his modest wage had been cut. The owner of the business where he worked said there was no choice. To keep the business's doors open, everyone would have to take a cut in pay. It was not clear that the owner would reduce his own compensation, but all the workers would see a reduction.

It was a particular blow to Millie and her family because not long before the doctor had told them that their child who was afflicted with a chronic illness would require constant medication. It was not cheap, and to afford it Millie had tightened the household budget strings. The family ate meat just two nights a week. She cut back the portions of grain meal she used for a main course at the other dinners of the week and added more water to keep the volume up. She always patched the family's clothes. Now she resolved to patch even the oldest and most threadbare ones that she had hoped to replace as the holidays drew near.

But something else happened too. Millie began to focus on her blessings. There were the few things she had. There was a nice silk scarf, as fine as any in the land, that Myra had given her. She never had occasion to wear it except when both families gathered once a year for the holidays. But she kept it in a drawer, and from time to time she would open the drawer, pick up the scarf, rub it against her cheek, and think of the deep love she and her sister shared. Millie also had an elegant parasol that her husband had bought for her in better days, which she kept behind the bedroom door. She considered it an extravagance when he purchased it, but she appreciated it as a reminder of her husband's deep love for her. She also cherished a special cup, not because it had any intrinsic value but because it had belonged to her dear mother.

She found great comfort in the assurance that things were of secondary value to her. When she could not replace her daughter's old cloak with another she had hoped by buy, she resolved to replace it with an extra hug each day. The smile on her daughter's face each time they shared a hug told Millie that she had made a sound compensation. And Millie found that the deliberate embrace renewed her.

Just the anticipation of her daughter's hug would bring a smile to her face as she prepared the first meal of the day while the children still slept. She felt an inner warmth against the drafts in her old house. She decided to stir the porridge with extra care each morn, replacing a cup of meal with a mother's love. If the children noticed that the cereal's texture had thinned, they said nothing.

She decided that a hug and soft kiss each morning would also help bolster her husband's spirit as he started out the door to a day of hard labor and uncertain rewards.

Like her sister, she went to the market each day. But they seldom saw each other because Millie browsed the area with the most modest stalls that sold only the most basic necessities. She also waited until late in the day, when the vendors were closing down. Selections were poor then. But the prices on what was left were minimal.

Sometimes she would be lucky enough to catch a vendor tossing away the last of his wilting produce. When that happened, she dashed to collect what she could. Sometimes the merchant mocked her and bystanders would even join in. But their harsh words couldn't dull the sense of good fortune she felt obtaining some foodstuffs for free. By the time she reached her home with the treasure, her heart would be so full of gratitude that she would be humming a sweet melody out loud.

If she heard herself humming, she might even break into song. Then it would seem as if the whole house would brighten up. The children would ask what prompted this special joyousness. And her husband would be curious too. But she would just smile and tell them that she was reflecting on and enjoying her blessings — the most precious of which were each of them.

Not all her days at the market were fortunate. Sometimes demand exceeded supplies and she returned home with only a meager handful of produce with which to supplement the porridge. Nevertheless, the walk home was always a graced moment because at the turn in the lane, just before it narrowed and started to climb the few blocks to their small home, she would meet the beggars.

They were people afflicted by all manner of misfortune, physical and mental and some even spiritual. They were always eager for a handout, and most of them were polite despite their desperate circumstances. Millie always held out at least one small piece of her market treasure for one of the beggars.

She relished the days when she could do more. On the days she foraged discarded produce, she filled her arms with as much as she could carry. The weight of the load was lightened by the thought of how much good her fortune would do for the beggars as well as her family.

Some days she would leave as much as half her bounty with the poor souls at the bottom of the lane — and feel grateful to the beggars for lightening her load. Then the sense of abundance she felt filled her up to overflowing.

Whatever she did or felt, Millie always kept her focus on how much she was blessed. Sometimes, when her supply was meager, it pained her not to be able to give the beggars more. But she always made it a point to be thankful for the opportunity to give whatever it was she could spare — and to be even more thankful for what she was taking home to her family. That made her mindful of her family, and that made her still more grateful.

In that way, by the time she returned from the market, no matter how large or how small the supply of produce she carried, her heart was filled with gratitude.

Throughout the evening she focused on the objects of her gratitude. She noticed when an eye twinkled or a dimple appeared. She tried not to miss a single smile on any face around the table. And she even gave thanks when she saw a brow furrow. It reminded her that her home was full of life — the most basic and very best reason to celebrate.

Darkness always came quickly and the family always retired soon after because oil for the lamps was a luxury. Millie passed the time from dusk to dark carefully tucking in each of her children, letting her hug linger while she reflected on how they were such miracles. She moved with purpose, but slowly, making sure she took the time to answer each question. She also took special care to encourage the children to expand their realms of concern and gratitude as they recited their prayers. It would not do for them to focus only on their own wants and needs.

She never failed to notice when her husband brought in a big load of firewood and banked the fire to keep it burning through the night. With her last ounce of energy and the last minute of waning light, she gently hugged and softly kissed him, and thanked him for working so hard and caring so much for his family.

Sometimes, when the news from work was particularly distressing, she held his head to her breast and softly ran her fingers through his hair while his tears flowed. On occasion, her tears would join his. But in a flash her heart would fill with gratitude for so many things — the time they had together, for his strength and the warmth of his tears, and for the children, from whom they wanted to spare any notion of heartbreak.

As she lay in their hard bed, bundled tight against the drafts, she had a choice: she could curse the drafts or celebrate the pile of worn blankets that covered them. She cuddled the blankets and offered prayers of gratitude for a husband who loved his family and gave them his best, for her children, for the covers over her shoulders and the roof over their head, for the fire in the fireplace across the room, for the meal and the opportunity her family had to share it together. The more she thought about these things, the more blessed she felt.

Always she smiled. And if sometimes tears slipped across her smile, nearly always they were tears of joy. Never once did she feel herself alone. As sleep closed in, her last thought would be eager anticipation of the morn, when she could greet her family and help them start the day. Before she could contemplate the details of a new day, she was embraced by the deep and restful sleep that comes to purposeful people grateful for the abundance of their lives.

34

9. Rich or Wealthy?

Suddenly Mr. Peabody sat up straight. His quick motion brought the twins back to the table. "Now you tell me, which of the sisters was wealthy?" he asked.

Olivia looked at Todd, who was looking back at her. Neither could read a clue on the other's face. Finally Olivia spoke. "Well, Myra had more money. That's obvious. But somehow, Mr. Peabody, I'm finding it hard to say she was wealthy."

"What about you, Todd?" Mr. Peabody asked.

"I'm with Olivia on this. Myra has a lot of stuff and Millie barely gets by. But I'm not comfortable saying Myra is the wealthy one. She's rich for sure, but she has so many concerns, so many needs, and so many things trouble her."

"Maybe it's time to define some terms," Mr. Peabody offered.

Neither of the twins had any idea how that was the least bit relevant. But they were happy to let Mr. Peabody take the lead. They both nodded their agreement.

"Good," Mr. Peabody continued. "Let's define rich as having a lot of things. And let's define wealthy as experiencing abundance — the sense that you have all that you need and more. Are you with me on this?" They both nodded again.

"Okay. If we use our definitions, who is the richest?" he asked.

"That's easy," said Todd. "Myra is the rich one."

36

"Yeah, but Millie is the wealthy one," Olivia interjected.

"Does that seem strange to you?" asked Mr. Peabody.

The twins were quiet for an instant before Todd spoke. "It's not something I ever thought about before," he said. "I mean, I've thought about being rich. But I've never thought about how a person could be rich but not wealthy — or the other way around, be wealthy but not rich. It's all a little strange when you think about it."

Olivia chimed in: "I've never thought about it this way either. I mean, I just treated rich and wealthy as the same thing. If you have a lot of stuff, you're rich and wealthy. That seemed pretty obvious. But now I'm not sure. I mean Myra is way more rich than Millie. But using your definition she's not wealthy at all. She's ... she's ... you know ... she's ... how do you say it?"

"She's impoverished? Is that the word?" Todd asked, looking at Mr. Peabody.

"That's a very good word, Todd," Mr. Peabody replied. "Because it comes from the notion of poverty, and maybe that's a good word to bring into our conversation about being wealthy. Let's talk for a moment about the difference between being wealthy and impoverished."

The twins nodded agreement.

"It seems to me," Mr. Peabody continued, "the big difference between being wealthy or impoverished is whether or not you have enough."

38

10. What is Enough?

"Mr. Peabody, I'm not sure what you mean by having enough," said Todd, "but I can see where how wealthy we are cannot be measured by the amount of money we have. Otherwise, Myra would be wealthy and Millie would be impoverished. But the strange thing is, Myra is rich but she doesn't feel wealthy. She feels impoverished."

"And Millie is poor but doesn't feel impoverished. She feels wealthy," Olivia chimed in.

"You're on the right track," said Mr. Peabody. "We know that the big distinction between being wealthy and being impoverished is not an exact amount of money — because having a lot of money does not necessarily make you feel wealthy."

"And if you don't feel wealthy, what good are your riches?" Todd asked rhetorically. "You can fill your bank account with money, you can fill your closet with fine clothes, you can fill your house with wonderful furniture, you can fill your garage with hot cars. But if that doesn't fill you up with joy, what's the point? How can you be satisfied, how can you be wealthy, if you have no sense of abundance?"

"It's clear that some people are rich and yet impoverished," Olivia offered. "And it's clear that riches — money or things — can't make you wealthy. In fact, as we saw in Myra's case, sometimes the more you have the more impoverished you become."

"Good insight!" Mr. Peabody said. "But we know even more than that, don't we?"

The twins looked quizzical. "We do?" asked Todd.

"Well, we know that someone is not made wealthy or impoverished by a specific amount of money. And we also know that someone is not made wealthy or impoverished on the basis of comparing their circumstances to the circumstances of others."

"We know that?" Olivia asked.

"Well, if we reflect on the story of Myra and Millie, I think we do," Mr. Peabody replied. "Otherwise, Myra could have just compared herself to her sister and decided she was wealthy."

"She didn't do that," Todd chimed in.

"But she did compare herself to others who had more things than she had and then decided she was impoverished," Olivia offered.

"Good point!" Mr. Peabody said. "Myra compared herself to people whose circumstances would make her feel impoverished, but she didn't compare herself to people whose circumstances could make her feel wealthy. Why do you think that happened?"

"I don't have a clue," said Olivia.

Todd thought he might. "It's like she was in a game, she had two ways to play the game, and she chose the way that she would lose. It doesn't make any sense, but I see how it could happen," he said. Suddenly he was out of words and short of ideas. "What's the answer, Mr. Peabody?"

"Well, one answer is we don't know exactly why she would do that," Mr. Peabody replied. "But we do know something else."

"What's that?" Olivia asked.

"We know that comparing ourselves to others isn't a good way to decide whether we are wealthy or impoverished," Mr. Peabody replied.

No matter how rich or poor we are ...
we will always be rich compared to some people ... and poor compared to others.

11. When Do We Have Enough?

"I have a question," Olivia said, looking at Mr. Peabody. "When you said 'the big difference between being wealthy and being impoverished is whether or not we have enough,' I was lost for a second. I wondered what does enough mean. Then I thought, enough is when you have as much as the other people around you, especially the ones you want to be like. So I started comparing, and that was pretty easy to do. But now I see the trouble that comparing caused Myra. So I agree with you that comparisons are not a good way to know if we are wealthy. But if that's true, how can we ever know if we have enough, and can we ever know if we are wealthy?"

"Great questions," said Mr. Peabody. "Let's start by defining enough. Let's say that having enough means having more than we need. Does that make sense?" The twins nodded.

"Okay, so being wealthy is having more than we need. Do you agree?" Mr. Peabody asked. Again the twins nodded.

"Now let's look a little closer at Myra's experience and see if we can't find an answer for your questions. There's something else we know about her that we haven't really discussed."

"What's that?" Todd asked.

"We know that Myra's experience of being impoverished was not really rooted in reality," Mr. Peabody explained. "Sure, she looked outside herself and found the evidence to convince herself that she was impoverished. But she saw only a small part of the whole picture. We don't know why she saw only the part that made her feel impoverished. But we still have a big clue here — because it's clear that her sense of being impoverished really came from inside her, from her focus rather than from the facts of life."

"You're right, Mr. Peabody!" Olivia almost shouted. "I like the way you can find clues even when you don't have an answer. I think that's pretty smart.

"Okay, time to recap," said Mr. Peabody. "We know the difference between being wealthy and being impoverished is whether or not you realize that you have enough. And we know that having enough means having more than you need. But we also know that it cannot be based on any exact amount of money or possessions, or on comparisons with others. The sense of whether or not we have enough — whether we are wealthy or impoverished — comes from somewhere inside each of us. Perhaps, then, it is a choice."

"A choice?" the twins asked in unison. "I thought I was following you, but maybe I wasn't," said Olivia. "Me too," echoed Todd. "Now I'm confused."

"I think you're doing fine," Mr. Peabody declared. "We're all on track."

"Yeah, but where are we going?" Todd asked impishly.

"We're going back to our basic distinction," said Mr. Peabody. "If the difference between being wealthy and impoverished is whether or not we have enough, we have to look again at the concept of enough. If we can't determine that by counting what we have or by comparing ourselves to others, how do we know when we have enough?"

"When you can't get any more in the garage," said Todd with a grin.

Mr. Peabody chuckled. "Maybe you're on to something. Maybe a person would have to conclude they have enough when they have no place left to put anything more."

"I was just kidding," Todd said. "I mean, if someone was rich they would just make their garage or house bigger, or buy a bigger house like Myra did, or maybe even build a warehouse. They could just keep adding on or moving so they would always have more room for more stuff."

"I think you've stumbled on something important," Mr. Peabody said.

"I have?" Todd asked, surprised and happy to be redeemed.

"You've made the point that the amount of stuff you accumulate — even the size of the house and the garage you have to put all the stuff in — isn't a good way to measure wealth," Mr. Peabody explained. "Since there is always more to get and more places to put all the stuff you get, if you distinguish between wealth and poverty on the basis of filling up to capacity with stuff, you will always be impoverished because your capacity is always expandable," he added. "So we return to our question: How do you know when you have enough?"

12. Enough to Share

The twins were quiet for a long time. They had no idea how to answer Mr. Peabody's question. Then something occurred to Olivia but she was reluctant to mention it. Finally she could not keep it in. "How about this, Mr. Peabody? Maybe you know that you have enough for yourself when you have enough to share." she said softly.

Mr. Peabody's eyes widened. "Say more about that, Olivia."

"Well, in one sense you can never have enough because there's always more to buy, more to have," she said, gaining confidence with every word. "And there's always more room to put it. You can buy more space — a bigger house and a bigger garage. There's no limit to what you can buy, really. So in one sense you would never have enough unless you had everything. And that's not going to happen because people are always making more — more things and more kinds of things.

"As Dad likes to say, there are always more toys to get," Todd chimed in. Olivia continued. "When you think of being wealthy as a matter of getting and having more, you can never have enough — so you can never be wealthy. But when you think of being wealthy as having more than you need, you can be sure that you're wealthy if you give some away and you're still okay."

Todd's eyes brightened. "That's interesting. If you focus on getting more so that you have enough, the gap between what you have and what you could have just keeps getting wider and wider. You never get any rest. You never find any peace. You never have lasting joy. But if you can give some things away and it doesn't destroy you, that tells you that you have more than you need. Then you can relax and start to enjoy what you have."

"The way to know you have more than you need," Olivia interjected, "is to know that you have something to share or something to spare. That tells you that you have a surplus. And that's good to know. I mean, it's proof that you have more than you need. When you know that, you can't help appreciating what you have. And that helps you focus on your abundance. You really do feel wealthy."

"And you feel happy," Todd added.

"So it's really happiness that people are after when they chase riches?" Mr. Peabody asked.

"I think it is," said Todd, a bit surprised by his own discovery.

Olivia wanted to continue with her line of thought: "Maybe you don't have enough to cover all your needs for another week or a month or a year or a lifetime. But when you stop to think about it, who really does? If you focus only on what you don't have or on what you could have, you are always in need of something. But if, instead, you give something away, it changes your focus. It tells you that you've got enough to get through the day and sleep pretty soundly that night. It gives you peace of mind you can't get any other way."

Suddenly she stopped. "Does this make any sense at all?"

"I think you're making a lot of sense," Mr. Peabody said.

13. Connecting to Purpose

Todd was still digesting the conversation. Finally he spoke. "But Olivia, what if someone only had a penny and wanted to feel rich, so she just gave it away and then she had nothing. Would that make her wealthy?"

Mr. Peabody interjected. "If she kept the penny, Todd, do you think she would be rich?"

"No," said Todd. "A penny can't buy hardly anything."

"So if she kept the penny, she would be poor by your definition?" Mr. Peabody asked, looking at Todd.

"Yeah, I guess so," said Todd.

"And do you think she would feel poor?" Mr. Peabody persisted.

"I think so," said Todd. "I mean, I sure would."

"Then, if she gave the penny away, it wouldn't make much difference to her circumstances?" Mr. Peabody asked.

"No, a penny can't buy anything," said Todd.

"So in one sense, it doesn't matter if she keeps the penny or gives it away. Either way, she's poor."

"I guess that's what I'm saying," Todd replied.

"But if she gave the penny away, how do you think she'd feel?"

"Destitute!" Todd replied, pleased with his own cleverness.

"Really?" Mr. Peabody asked, a smile beginning to creep across his face.

Todd knew he was trapped. "No. I mean, she would be destitute. But she'd probably feel pretty good, especially if she gave the penny to some good cause."

"Okay, then, if giving away her last cent could make a desperately poor person feel good, how do you think giving away a little more than that would make the average person feel?" Mr. Peabody asked.

Olivia and Todd looked at each other. Finally, Olivia spoke. "I think it would make them feel good too," she said.

"Yeah," Todd chimed in. "If your need is to get things, that is just going to eat away at you. And you won't ever be happy for very long. People who have a lot of needs aren't happy, no matter how much stuff they have.

"But if you give something away for a good cause, you know that you have accomplished something," he continued. "You have made someone else happy. I think you could feel good about that for a long, long time. You know, it's like if you get yourself a t-shirt, you end up with another t-shirt. No big deal! But if you give your money to help a poor child get a t-shirt, it's like you're helping to clothe the naked. That's a bigger deal, so it makes you feel good."

"Are you suggesting," Mr. Peabody asked "that it's easier to help others than to satisfy the self?"

"I've never thought of it that way before," said Todd. "But I know that when you help others, it's like you're connected to a bigger purpose. You're really doing something important. Even if your particular part is pretty small — maybe even just a penny, if that's all you have — you still feel like you are part of something bigger. Because you are connected to important accomplishments, your life begins to mean something. You feel that your life has some significance."

"Can you think of an example?" Mr. Peabody asked.

"I can," said Olivia. "When I saved some of my lunch money for weeks and weeks to help families recover from a hurricane in Central America, I felt really good about it. I mean, I didn't like going without a candy bar after lunch. The first day was really hard. After that, some days were easy and some were almost impossible. In fact, once I couldn't resist. Okay, twice. But it really felt good most of the time. Even if I missed my candy bar, it still felt good to be part of something important like that. You know, it still does. I feel good knowing that I helped kids and their parents get their lives back together. In fact, the only thing I still feel a little bad about were those two times I couldn't resist."

"Don't you regret going without the candy bars on all the days that you were able to deprive yourself?" Mr. Peabody asked.

"At the time I sometimes really did," Olivia confessed. "I obsessed about it for a few minutes, maybe even a couple of hours. But it doesn't matter now. In fact, it felt good to know I could get by without a candy bar at the end of lunch. Later in the year, I used that knowledge to save up some money to get some earrings that I wanted — so now that I think about it, my little sacrifice made me richer in two ways. It helped me contribute to an important cause and it helped me learn that I have some choices with my candy money. I don't have to just use it to buy one candy bar a day. I can save it up for bigger things — for me or for others. That's good to know," Olivia said, smiling because she had just learned something from listening to herself.

"Ah hah," Mr. Peabody jumped in. "I think you are making my point for me. But first let me clarify something. Are you saying that even while you were in the process of being able to give something away, you were getting something for yourself too?" Mr. Peabody asked.

Olivia twisted her face a bit. She wasn't sure what Mr. Peabody was trying to say.

He saw her confusion and tried again. "You said that while you were saving up to help children and their families rebuild their lives, you also learned that you had some choices in life that you didn't know you had before. And later you applied what you learned to make the choice to get some earrings you wanted. So you got knowledge and you got earrings — in addition to getting the satisfaction of connecting and contributing to a big, important cause that did some people a lot of good. Is that what you're saying?"

"I guess I am!" said Olivia, relieved that Mr. Peabody did not ask her a hard question.

"And that's my point exactly," Mr. Peabody declared.

Both Olivia and Todd furrowed their brows and asked in the same breath, "What is? What's your point?"

"Generosity is powerful medicine that tastes good," Mr. Peabody replied.

Olivia and Todd smiled in wonder at the thought.

Mr. Peabody started to get up from the table. "We've

discovered a lot today but I've got to run now," he said. "Hope I see you soon. Maybe we can continue this then." He was out of earshot in an instant, but he turned back briefly to wave.

"We better get going, too," Olivia said, looking at the clock on the wall. "Mom's going to be worrying about us if we're not back before dinner."

The twins got up and headed toward the door. On their way home they didn't talk at all. Instead, they both contemplated Mr. Peabody's point.

Generosity is powerful medicine

... that tastes good.

14. Worth the Wait

The twins were busy all week, but that only fed their interest in seeing Mr. Peabody on Saturday morning. Their mom always had chores for them to do first thing after breakfast. She was surprised when they listened attentively to her list at the breakfast table and proceeded to tackle all the jobs immediately after they ate.

In no time at all the twins were standing over her. "Can we go down to the bookstore now?" asked Olivia. "We're all done with all our chores."

"Already?" asked their mother, a bit incredulous that they would have completed everything in less than an hour. "I'm amazed. Are you sure your rooms are going to pass inspection? You haven't been at it very long."

"I did everything you said just exactly how you told me to do it," said Olivia.

"My room is spotless too," said Todd. "I did it right this time. Now can we go to the bookstore?"

"Okay," their mother replied. "But be home by noon for lunch."

They had almost cleared the backyard by the time their mother finished her sentence. "Thanks," shouted Todd, on the run.

"We'll be back by noon," added Olivia, jogging at his heels.

They kept up their brisk pace and in a few minutes they were pushing through the bookstore's door and heading directly for Mr. Peabody's favorite booth. He was reading a book as the twins approached.

"Hi, Mr. Peabody," Todd said.

"What are you doing?" asked Olivia.

"I'm waiting for you two so we can continue our discussion about being rich and being wealthy," he replied.

The twins slid into the booth across from him, eager for the discussion to begin.

Mr. Peabody smiled gently, took a moment to look into each of the twins' eyes, and asked, "What do you think?"

"About what?" Olivia asked.

"About being rich and being wealthy," Mr. Peabody replied.

"Our last discussion has me wondering about a lot of things," said Todd. "I have always thought the more money you have, the wealthier you are and the happier you are. But now I don't think that's true."

"Being rich may be about how much money you have, but I think being wealthy is way more important — and that's about focus," said Olivia. "I mean, if you look at the story of Myra and Millie, it's clear that Myra is rich — but she's also miserable because her focus is on all the things she doesn't have. Meanwhile, Millie is poor but she lives a life full of abundance and joy because her focus is on what she does have. It doesn't matter that she has less materially than her sister because her sister is blind to what she has."

"You could say Millie is blind too," said Todd. "I mean,

she doesn't seem to notice all the things she doesn't have. What's the difference?"

"The huge difference is that Myra is miserable and Millie is happy," said Olivia. "If Millie is blind to her poverty, you get the impression that this is her choice — that she chooses to focus on the few but important things she has and be happy instead of focusing on the many things she doesn't have and being miserable. I admire that. But it's hard to believe that Myra's blindness is the result of the same kind of choice because it makes her miserable — and why would anyone choose that?"

"I get it," said Todd. "So long as my focus is on getting things for myself, I can never be wealthy because I would always run out of money before I run out of things to buy."

"Good insight," said Mr. Peabody. "As long as we focus on obtaining things with our money, we can never be wealthy — because we will always run out of money before we run out of things to buy."

Olivia had been listening a little and thinking a lot. "I think being truly wealthy means that we have more than we need. But if we focus only on our desires and let them grow into needs, we will never have more than we need. So having stuff and getting more stuff are not good ways to measure if we have more than we need."

"Another good insight," said Mr. Peabody.

"All this talk about getting things takes me back to Christmas," said Todd. "Before Christmas we start thinking about what we want for presents. Then we go through the catalogs looking for the stuff we want. We find those things. But we also see a lot of things we hadn't thought about before — and then we want those things, too.

"And the more we think about it, the more we think we really need all those things," Olivia added.

"Like just before last Christmas I was looking through a catalog and saw a model airplane that really could fly," Todd continued. "When I saw it, I wanted it. And the more I thought about it, the more I wanted it. By Christmas morning I really needed it — because when it wasn't under the tree, I was disappointed. Can you imagine? Looking back, I got a lot of great things and it was a wonderful Christmas. But after we opened our presents, I felt badly all day because I didn't get that airplane. Apparently, I had made it a need — because I needed it to be happy. Hmm, I never understood it that way until I just said it. Do you get what I mean?"

"Absolutely!" said Mr. Peabody.

Olivia was absolutely ready to talk. "That happens to me, too. I want something. When I'm begging Mom to buy it, I even say, 'Mom, I need it. I really need it.' I mean that when I say it — even if it's something pretty silly. The more I beg or even think about the thing, the more I need to have it."

"I've heard a saying that describes what you and Todd are talking about," said Mr. Peabody.

Wants quickly grow up to be needs.

15. An Agent for Change

"I've got a question for you," Mr. Peabody said. "If we can only be wealthy when we have more than we need, and if our needs can grow without limit, does that mean we can never be wealthy?"

The twins thought about this for a good long while. It was nearly a minute before Olivia spoke. "That's a hard question, Mr. Peabody. But I think I have an answer. I think you can be wealthy. But I don't think you can be wealthy in the sense that you can get everything you need and want. Because, as we said before, no matter how much money you have, there's always more to want."

"And if there's more to want, there's more to need — because wants quickly grow up to be needs," Todd chimed in.

Olivia continued: "If your understanding of being wealthy is being able to buy everything you need or want, you are never going to be wealthy because you will always need or want more. But if your idea of being wealthy is to have more than you need, then I think there's a way to be wealthy."

"And how's that?" asked Mr. Peabody.

Olivia was pleased to continue. "We talked about this a little bit the last time, but I've been giving it a lot more thought. If your idea of being wealthy is to have more than you need, you will know you are wealthy when you give something away and you are still okay. Giving something away tells you that you don't really need it to live. When you know that, it's clear to you that you have more than you need. Maybe that's the first step to being wealthy."

Mr. Peabody smiled but no one spoke for a few moments. Then Todd said very softly. "Interesting. Very interesting. When you give something away and you're still okay, it tells you that you have more than you need — that you have a surplus. And if you experience a surplus, you are experiencing abundance. That could be the key. Is that the key, Mr. Peabody?"

He was not ready to answer the question directly, but he knew it was time to say something. "Let's answer my question first. When we change our minds do we change our habits?"

The twins looked at each other. Olivia spoke first. "I suppose we do. How else would we change if we didn't change our minds first?" she replied.

"Do you think it ever happens the other way around?" Mr. Peabody asked. "Could what we do affect how we think? Could we change our habits to change our minds?"

"I've never thought about it," said Todd.

"Me neither," said Olivia. "What do you think about it, Mr. Peabody?"

He seldom answered questions directly, but he knew it was time to do that now. "We don't think about it, but it happens all the time," Mr. Peabody replied. For example, I know you and Olivia never fight. But could it hypothetically happen that someday you're just feeling cranky, Todd, and she says something and suddenly you yell at her?"

"If you turn it around so she's cranky, it doesn't have to be hypothetical," Todd answered. Olivia jabbed him in the ribs.

Mr. Peabody continued: "Okay, let's say one of you is cranky and so you overreact and yell over a minor thing that on most days wouldn't anger you. Then your mother walks in the room and asks you why you yelled. What do you tell her? Do you say that you're just cranky?"

Olivia spoke first. "I would probably have all sorts of reasons for what I did. I'd tell my mom how Todd was teasing me, he's always teasing me. And I might even blame her too, especially if she didn't take my side. I guess I would have all sorts of reasons for doing what I did — not even counting the real reason you gave, which is that I was cranky."

Mr. Peabody raised his hands up off the table, always a sign of deep pleasure. "Exactly!" he said. "You would have all sorts of reasons to explain your behavior. We call these justifications. And when your mind starts to come up with them, we call that rationalizing. We do it all the time. Rationalization is a big word. It refers to our effort to have our behavior make sense to us and others."

Mr. Peabody continued: "Sometimes we act impulsively, without thinking. But if someone asks us why we did what we did, we come up with a reason — usually instantly. But it's a reason we came up with after we acted. That's a rationalization. At a deeper level, rationalization also refers to the fact that we are always trying to manufacture reasons for our behavior. As you noted before, Olivia, sometimes we will adopt an attitude change and then our behavior will change. But more often we manufacture a rationalization for doing something after we have already done it."

"Are you saying we make excuses for ourselves?" asked Olivia.

"We do that all the time," said Todd.

"Yes, we do," said Mr. Peabody. "But once we realize how the process works we can put it to use to achieve powerful change in our lives. In fact, it's how we unlock the Secret of Wealth."

"I don't understand," said Olivia.

"Let me explain," Mr. Peabody replied. "Our minds hunger for consistency. So when we change our minds, it can motivate us to change our behavior. But usually our motivation is very weak. What we don't notice is how the process works the other way around — and generally better — if we start by focusing on behavior. When our circumstances change or we act on impulse, our behavior changes. Then our minds change too — to justify our behavior. That way, what we are doing makes sense to us. Our behavior and our attitude are consistent. Most of the time this happens without us giving it any conscious thought at all."

"That scares me," Olivia cut in.

"How so?" Mr. Peabody asked.

"I want to think that I choose all of my attitudes and that controls my behavior. How I think and what I do should be my choices," she explained.

"Of course," Mr. Peabody said, smiling. "How we think is always our choice. But our choice is not always a conscious one. In fact, whenever we don't consciously choose how we think, then we unconsciously choose. It happens all the time. The fact is, if we want to consciously choose our attitudes and stick to our choices, then we have to enlist our behavior to help us."

"What do you mean?" Todd asked.

Mr. Peabody replied, "There's a powerful dynamic at work in every human being. Here is one way to explain it. When we want to bring about change in our lives, we can and we should consciously focus our minds on changing our behavior. But our minds are naturally focused on explaining our behavior — on rationalizing it. When we start with a change of attitude and don't focus on changing our behavior, our minds continue to defend — to rationalize — the old behavior we say we want to change. Pretty soon we talk ourselves out of the change we thought we wanted. Of course, we always find good reasons — excuses, really — for not changing. In the end, we spend a lot more time and energy trying to justify our behavior than we do trying to change it."

"Is that why it's so hard for people to change?" Olivia wondered out loud. She was thinking about how her father struggled to quit smoking and how she never seemed to be able to keep her room clean, which was embarrassing when her friends came by to visit.

"That's a big part of the reason," said Mr. Peabody. "Our minds think they are being kind to us by trying to justify everything we do. And, in fact, that is a benefit — until we want to change. Then it becomes a heavy burden — like pushing a big rock up a steep hill. Fortunately, we have two tools to help us. Regrettably, people have forgotten how to use the most powerful tool — their behavior. We often think that attitudes change behavior. But what we also have to remember is this:

Behavior changes attitudes.

16. The Lesson of the Line

"Let's head further down the Path of Questions," Mr. Peabody suggested. Both twins nodded. Sometimes they just wanted answers. But the Path of Questions was fun to walk. They always learned something new. And it was strange how this happened. They didn't learn new facts. Instead, they just connected things they already knew in new ways — and suddenly they knew something they didn't know before. It was exciting to learn new things simply by connecting things they already knew. It made the twins feel smart about themselves, and they liked that a lot.

"First, can you picture a line of five people?" Mr. Peabody asked. "At the left end is a man whose clothes are tattered and his old, cracked shoes are too big for him. At the other end is a woman. She has on a beautiful long gown and is wearing gold jewelry. What can we guess about them?"

"The woman is rich," said Olivia.

"And the man is poor," said Todd.

"Okay," said Mr. Peabody. "Now picture all the people in the line. Going from the poor man on the left to the rich woman on the right, each person is dressed a little better to indicate they are a little richer. Can you picture that?" Mr. Peabody asked.

Both twins smiled and nodded.

"All of these people need basic things to live. They need food, shelter and clothing. Can you think of anything else that they need just to survive?" Mr. Peabody asked.

The twins shook their heads. They could think of nothing more.

"Would you think that these basics — food, shelter and clothing — cost the same for all of them?" Mr. Peabody asked.

"They could," said Olivia, "but I don't think so. I think the ones on the right will go out to eat more, so they will spend more on food. They will have bigger and nicer homes that cost more, so they'll spend more on shelter too."

"And it's pretty obvious that the richer ones will spend more on clothes too," Todd added.

"Good," said Mr. Peabody. "I think we have a pretty good picture in our minds of these people's circumstances. So we agree that the more money these people have, the more they will spend on food, shelter and clothing. Now what about how much they have left over? Who has the most money left over after they pay for the basics?" Mr. Peabody asked.

"I think the woman on the right will have more left over too," said Olivia without hesitating. "I mean, she will spend more on the basics, but she will still have more left over after the basics, too."

"I agree," said Todd. "In fact, if the man on the left is very, very poor, he might not have enough money for all the basics. Maybe he couldn't afford any shelter and he's homeless."

"Right," Mr. Peabody said. "He could be so poor that he's homeless. But let's assume for the purposes of our exploration that the poorest man can afford some sort of shelter. Okay, so can we agree that the richer these people are, the more money they will spend on the basics — and yet the more money they will also have left over after that?" Mr. Peabody asked. The twins nodded their agreement.

"What people have left over is called discretionary income," Mr. Peabody explained. "That means it is money we have some choice about spending or saving after we have paid for our basics." The twins repeated the term and then Mr. Peabody continued.

"Okay, another question. Who has the most extra money that they could just give away if they wanted to?" Mr. Peabody asked.

"The rich woman way over on the right has the most," said Todd.

"And the man on the left has the least," said Olivia.

"Now," asked Mr. Peabody, "do you two understand percentages?"

"Of course," said Olivia, trying to sound like a fully grown up person.

"Good," said Mr. Peabody. "Now I want to ask you a question about percentages. Who has the highest percentage of discretionary income — money that they could give away if they wanted to?"

"That's easy," said Olivia. "The rich woman on the right has the highest percentage of discretionary income. If the man on the left has just enough money to get food, shelter and clothing, he has zero percent discretionary income and he can't afford to give any amount away."

"Okay, let's assume that's the case," Mr. Peabody said. "The man on the left has no money left over after he takes care of his basic needs. So we say he has zero percent discretionary income. After he provides for his basic needs at the most basic level, he is tapped out." The twins nodded in agreement.

"And let's assume that the woman on the right has so much money that after she provides for her basic needs, even in an elegant way, she still has 95 percent of her money left over as discretionary income. She can choose to spend it, save it, or give it away — or do all those things in any combination. Is that clear?" The twins nodded again.

"Now let's talk about the three people in the middle. For the sake of our conversation, let's say that the person next to the poorest man in line is a woman. If she scrimps, she has 10% discretionary income — money to use as she wants after covering her most basic needs. We'll say she's in the lower middle class category. Then let's assume the person to the right of her is a man, and he has 20% discretionary income. As far as our line goes, he's right in the middle, so we'll call him middle class. And let's assume the next person to the right is a woman and she has 30% discretionary income. For the purposes of our lineup, she's upper middle class. Are we clear on that?" Mr. Peabody asked. Again the twins nodded in agreement.

"Based on national studies, who will give the highest percentage of their income away to charity?" Mr. Peabody asked.

"I think the richest woman will give the most money," said Todd. "But I'm not sure about the highest percentage. If she's as rich as you say, Mr. Peabody, she can give a lot away and it still won't be a very big percentage of her discretionary income."

"Could it be the one in the middle?" asked Olivia, looking for a safe guess.

"It could," said Mr. Peabody. "But it generally isn't."

"Then I think it's the woman you called upper middle class," guessed Todd. "She has a lot of money left over after paying for her basics, so she could give away a good bit of money. But since she's not outrageously rich, what she gives could be the highest percentage of the people in the line."

"It could, Todd," said Mr. Peabody. "But it's not."

"If we eliminate the poor man because he has nothing to give away after he covers his basics, the only one we haven't guessed yet is the woman who you called lower middle class," Todd said.

"And that's probably the right answer," Mr. Peabody said. "What we know for sure is that either the poor person or the lower middle class person will give the largest percentage of their income to charity — even though they have the smallest percentage of discretionary income left over after they cover the basics."

"Why is that?" asked Olivia, shocked that the poor man would or could give anything away.

"The short answer is that we don't know," Mr. Peabody replied. The twins sunk in their booth, obviously disappointed.

"But what we don't know is still helpful to us in understanding the Secret of Wealth," Mr. Peabody said.

"How can something we don't know help us to know more about something else?" asked Olivia, skeptical of Mr. Peabody's optimism.

Mr. Peabody smiled and chuckled. He liked to see young people develop their critical thinking skills. To him a little skepticism was a sign of deep inner growth. "Good question, Olivia. Now I think it's my turn to illustrate an answer for you." That prompted both twins to sit up and lean across the table toward Mr. Peabody. He had their undivided attention.

17. Getting More, Having Less

"What we see and know about our line of people tells us something profound about the Secret of Wealth," Mr. Peabody began. "Let's start with some small things and build from there. First, we know that poorer people spend a higher percentage of their income on charity than do wealthier people — even though we know they have to spend a higher percentage of their income just to cover the basics of living. One of the things that should tell us is that no matter how poor we are, almost all people in our country can find a little surplus — a little money left over — to help others in need. Very few people are so poor they have nothing to share. And, in fact, even the poorest can and do help each other in other ways. They give what time and talents they have to helping each other."

The twins nodded to show they understood.

"But we also see that as people get more income, two things happen. First, they need to spend a smaller percentage on the basics, so they have a larger percentage of discretionary income that theoretically they could give away. But second, instead of giving away a larger percentage of their income, they give away a smaller percentage. So as people get more, they actually give less of it away."

The twins looked at each other in surprise.

Mr. Peabody continued: "Yet, we know that most people like to do good things and like to help one another. In fact, I looked it up this morning and learned that people in 89% of all households in our country contribute money to some good cause. It must be satisfying or so many people wouldn't do it. So how do you explain why as our income goes up the portion that we give to help others goes down?" Mr. Peabody asked.

The twins looked perplexed. Finally Olivia spoke. "When I was a kid, I really didn't believe it when my grandmother said it was more blessed to give than to receive. I figured she said that because all she got for Christmas were scarves and pins. If that's all I got, getting things wouldn't be blessed at all. But then my class adopted a family for Christmas, and we started saving and planning what we would get them. And you know what? It really did make my Christmas special. I don't know if it was more blessed to give than to receive because I still really, really like getting stuff. But it was pretty special."

"Yeah," Todd agreed. "It was pretty special. It made me think that when I get big I want to be able to help more people."

"Whenever I hear people talking about winning a big lottery prize, they almost always mention doing something to help others," Mr. Peabody said. "I'm convinced that almost all of us care about others and want to help people in need. So it's a puzzle why as people move up the economic ladder, they give less of what they have to charity. I think the only explanation is that they think they can't afford it. They look at their needs and they look at their income, and they conclude that they don't have very much money left over."

"Are they wrong?" Todd wondered out loud.

"No, Todd, they're not wrong — at least not in one sense," Mr. Peabody replied. "They're competent with their money. They know how much they take in, so they know how much they can afford to spend on basics and then on discretionary things. But the interesting thing is that as they earn more and more, they look at their income and conclude that they have less and less of it left over to give away. In terms of money, we know they're getting richer, but how do you think they feel? Do you think they feel wealthy?"

"Obviously they feel poorer," said Olivia, scrunching up her face to make it clear she didn't understand why that would be. "That doesn't seem fair."

Mr. Peabody chuckled. "No, it doesn't, does it?

"It doesn't make sense either," said Todd, "Are you saying that as people get more money they end up feeling poorer instead of wealthier?"

"That's exactly what I'm saying!" Mr. Peabody replied. "I agree with you both: it doesn't seem fair and it doesn't make sense. But it happens all the time. So my next question is: Who is responsible when this happens?"

The twins weren't expecting a question like that. The questions that Mr. Peabody asked them were usually very easy to answer — almost obvious. This one required some deep thinking.

Finally Olivia went looking for some help. "Are you asking who is responsible for a person getting more money but feeling like they are poorer?"

"I am," said Mr. Peabody, smiling broadly. The twins just sat in the booth across from Mr. Peabody, their backs slouched and their brows furrowed. This was a hard question.

Finally Todd spoke. "I guess," he said haltingly, "if a person gets more money but feels like he has less, he is responsible for feeling that way. I mean, you can't blame it on the amount of money he has, because that amount is more, not less. So how he feels is up to him."

"Excellent!" said Mr. Peabody. "How he feels is his choice, even though he might not be aware of it. Next question: If a person gets more money but feels like he has less, what does that tell us?"

This question was more difficult than the last. The twins didn't know what to say. "Please tell us," Olivia pleaded. "If a person gets more money but feels like he or she has less, what does that tell us?"

Mr. Peabody was ready to continue. "If a person gets more money but feels like he has less, it confirms for us that the amount of money a person has does not determine if they are truly wealthy. Let me put that another way: The amount of money a person has is not the key that unlocks the Secret of Wealth.

"In fact," he continued, "we have seen that as people get more money, they're tempted to focus more on the things they don't have — things they could have if they just had more money. Of course, this means they are less focused on the things they do have, so their sense of abundance decreases. That's how it can happen that as people get more money they feel less and less wealthy. But in the end it's a choice, isn't it?"

The twins looked at one another. They were not sure if they understood what Mr. Peabody was saying but they wanted to be absolutely clear about it. "Are you saying that being wealthy is more about focus and choice than about how much money we make or pile up?" asked Todd.

Mr. Peabody smiled. "Yes, Todd, exactly," he replied. "I'm saying:

Wealth is more
about focus
than about
money

... and focus is
a choice.

18. Where Do We Live?

Olivia was skeptical. "Why would feeling poor be a choice?" she finally asked. "I mean, why would anyone — especially rich people — make that choice if they really thought about it?"

"But that's the point, isn't it, Mr. Peabody?" Todd chimed in. "People make the choice without thinking about it. We're talking about a choice people make unconsciously because they don't focus and make a conscious choice."

"Exactly!" Mr. Peabody proclaimed. "Remember, either we consciously make our choices or we unconsciously make them — and when we unconsciously make them it's as if they are made for us. Many people unconsciously choose to feel poorer, even as their income is increasing, because they don't consciously choose to focus on their wealth. If they don't acknowledge their abundance, they can't recognize it. And if they can't recognize it, they can't embrace it or nurture it. They can't increase it. And they certainly can't enjoy it!"

Mr. Peabody continued: "No matter how much more money they make, these people are never going to become wealthy. It may be obvious to everyone else that they are rich. But since they don't experience abundance, they have no sense of being wealthy. In fact, because of their focus, like Myra they can become ever more impoverished even as their income keeps going up and up."

"That sounds sad," said Olivia very softly. "I mean, these people are probably working harder and harder and feeling ever more pressure to earn more and more money

— but it doesn't matter because unless they change their focus they will never, ever be wealthy."

"It is sad, Olivia," Mr. Peabody agreed. "But I know many people who are stuck in that situation. As a friend of mine puts it, they are holed up in Scarcity when they could be living in Abundance. And the only thing that move requires is a change in focus."

"But not everyone is going to be wealthy just by changing the way they look at things," Todd objected. "I mean, the poor man at the left end of our line is poor no matter what he thinks."

"You have a good point, Todd, as far as it goes," Mr. Peabody replied. "By no external measures is the man at the left of the line rich. He has barely enough to get by, to provide the basics for himself. So by no empirical measure can we say he is rich. But let me ask you a question. Do you think it's possible that he could be happier than the other persons in the line?"

"Maybe," said Todd, his voice full of doubt.

Mr. Peabody continued his line of questioning. "If he was happier, could we say his life was more enriched than the others?"

"I guess we could," said Todd. "Even though he is poor, he could be happier than the others. But I don't think you could ever say he was rich, much less wealthy," said Todd.

"For the moment, let me agree with you and say that the man's circumstances are so meager that we cannot consider him either rich or wealthy," Mr. Peabody replied. "But let me ask you this. If we both agree that he could be happy in his circumstances, does it make any sense for the others with more to feel impoverished?"

"I guess not," Todd said.

"So let's focus on those people who have more than they need to provide for their basics and yet are filled with the feeling that they don't have enough. Where do they live?" Mr. Peabody asked.

"They live in Scarcity," said Olivia, happy to be part of the conversation again.

"Right, they live in Scarcity," said Mr. Peabody. "And do they live there because they want to?" he asked.

"I don't think so," said Olivia. Todd had to agree. "No, I don't think they want to be there. I don't think anyone does," he said.

"Okay," said Mr. Peabody, "we have established that they are living in Scarcity and that they don't want to live there. And, as we said before, they could leave Scarcity and live in Abundance without even having to pack up or move anything but their focus. So why don't they do it?" the old man asked.

The twins looked at each other. Finally, Olivia couldn't take the silence any longer. "We don't know, Mr. Peabody. Why don't they just do it?"

"Because they can't," Mr. Peabody replied. His tone was so matter of fact it sounded indifferent, almost mean.

"They can't?" Olivia asked incredulously. "I thought it was a choice. I thought it was easy to live in Abundance instead of Scarcity."

Mr. Peabody put up his hand as if to tell Olivia to slow

down. She began again, slower and more softly, "I thought it was a choice. I thought it was as easy as changing your mind."

"Well, it is a choice," said Mr. Peabody. "It's a matter of changing one's mind. But it isn't easy. In fact, for many, it's so difficult that it seems impossible."

"If it's impossible how can it be a choice?" asked Todd.

"I didn't say it was impossible. I only said it seems impossible to some people," Mr. Peabody explained. "As a matter of fact, it's very possible. But it's possible only if you use both tools we talked about."

"You mean attitude and behavior?" Olivia asked.

"That's exactly what I mean," Mr. Peabody replied. "To be wealthy, to really know and to actually benefit from the Secret of Wealth, you have to live in Abundance instead of Scarcity. That move isn't a physical move. You don't change addresses. Instead, it's a mental move. To move from Scarcity to Abundance, all you have to do is change your focus. But to change your focus, you have to use the tool of behavior. You have to live in Abundance."

"What do you mean by that?" Todd asked.

"It's only after you are living in Abundance that you gradually discover you have made the move from Scarcity," Mr. Peabody replied.

"I don't get it," Todd said. "How can you live in a place before you move to that place? Don't you move first, and then live where you have moved to?"

"When you're talking about the objective, physical world that we share, you're right, Todd," Mr. Peabody replied. "In that world, change begins with an idea. You get the idea to move from one city to the next, then you do it, and after that you are living in a new place. But in the mental worlds that we each construct for ourselves — the worlds where we find meaning — it's the other way around. Deep change often begins with action — a behavior you repeat over and over again. This behavior changes the way you are living and challenges your mind to construct reasons for the change — to rationalize the change.

"Remember, change itself can be good or bad, intended or accidental. Either way, our mind tries to construct reasons for it," Mr. Peabody continued. "That's why people who slip into bad habits nearly always come up with what they consider good reasons for what they're doing — even if the behavior is harmful to them.

"We generally assume that our thoughts direct our behaviors. That's why we consider ourselves rational. But, in fact, we often act on impulse and on emotions, without a lot of thought. Then our minds devote a lot of time and energy to making sense of our behaviors — no matter how bizarre they might be. As I said before, this activity is called rationalization. Our minds have great power to rationalize, and while we usually employ this power to justify ourselves, no matter what we're doing, we can also use it to liberate ourselves and improve our lives."

The children looked confused, so Mr. Peabody continued trying to explain how changes in behavior can help bring about changes in attitude.

"We like to think that if we change our minds we will change our actions. But if that were true, there would be no such thing as a failed diet or a broken New Year's resolution," Mr. Peabody said.

"Mom would like that!" Olivia exclaimed. "She's always going on a diet, but it never seems to make any difference."

"And if New Year's resolutions always stuck, Dad would get the Christmas decorations off the roof before March — and that would make Mom double happy," Todd added.

Mr. Peabody laughed. "You get the point. When we assume that simply changing our attitudes will also change our actions, we miss a powerful step in achieving permanent change. We forget that our behavior shapes and changes our attitude. In fact, it's only after our attitude changes to rationalize a new behavior that we actually start to see a permanent change in ourselves and in our lives. So when we want to see change in our lives, we have to remember this, he said: "Without a deliberate change in our behavior we cannot achieve a lasting change in our attitudes."

19. Lasting Change

"I'm not sure I understand your point," Todd said. "Are you sure you don't have it backwards? Doesn't a change in behavior come as a result of a change in our attitude?"

"In a sense that's true," Mr. Peabody replied. "The change process begins with us wanting to change. Generally we express it as a hope or a goal. We want to achieve something or we want to quit doing something. Either way, that's a change in attitude. But what we have to remember is that it's a temporary change in attitude — usually a very temporary change. At a deeper level our mind wants consistency, and at the start of the change process it is focused on rationalizing what we have been doing all along. So at one level we want change. But at another, deeper level we resist change. And usually our resistance wins. To tip the balance and achieve deep, lasting change, we have to deliberately change our behavior, stick with that change no matter what our mind tells us, and eventually force it to rationalize our new behavior. Once we realize that behavioral change is at the root of lasting change in our lives, we unleash a powerful tool to achieve whatever it is that we want. Behavior is the best tool we have to move from Scarcity to Abundance."

"You make it sound so simple," said Olivia.

"It is simple," said Mr. Peabody. "But it's not easy."

He continued: "During that period when we are changing our behavior to achieve a lasting change in our outlook, our behavior and our attitudes are not consistent. Since the mind longs for consistency, it tries to undermine our efforts to change. That's why people fail so often. They do not stick to their new behavior during this transition period. They lose sight of their new goal or they convince themselves it is too difficult or not important. The mind has many tactics to resist change, so we have to persist in our new behavior for a long time before the mind comes around and begins to support and rationalize that behavior."

"Maybe that explains why Mom and Dad have such a hard time losing weight," said Todd. "They make that resolution every January 1. But by every Valentine's Day, they are off their diets and back to their old ways. Dad says he's lost 200 pounds — but it's the same 10 pounds 20 times over."

Mr. Peabody was pleased that the twins were beginning to come up with their own examples of his principle.

"You know," he said, "there's a law of physics that says a body at rest remains at rest unless acted upon by an outside force. It's that way with personal change, too. Usually we change in response to a force exerted by other people. But we can also exert outside force on ourselves by sticking to a new behavior until our mind quits fighting it and starts defending it. That's how we move from Scarcity to Abundance. And that's the basis for the Secret of Wealth.

"If you want to experience wealth, you must live in Abundance," Mr. Peabody continued. "The only way to get there is to become convinced that we have more than we need. And the best way to do that is to become a giver. Once we give a bit away and it doesn't make us destitute, we begin to realize that we have more than we absolutely need. It's only then that we can begin to experience the joy and peace of mind that true wealth provides. There's a quick way to explain this: Generosity fosters abundance."

20. The Simple Secret

Olivia and Todd were quiet for what seemed like a long time to them. Finally, Olivia spoke. "If you asked me yesterday, I would have said it the other way around: Abundance fosters generosity. I mean, when you get a lot, why not share some? But I think I am beginning to see your point."

"So do I," said Todd. "I was just thinking, if I want to be a basketball player, the only way to become one is to play the game. If I am not tall or I am not fast, I might never be good enough to turn pro or play in college or even make my high school team. But the only way for me to be the best basketball player that I can be is to go out and play the game. I change my behavior first, I live as a player, and eventually I do become the best player that I can be."

"Good example," Mr. Peabody said. "Of course, the process starts in the mind with a goal. But once we have a goal, we have to change our behavior and then stick to our new behavior. Be assured, our minds will work on us to give it up. But if we persist in our behavior, our minds will gradually change and begin defending and encouraging our new behavior instead of trying to undermine it. In the case of basketball, once you start playing you become a player. Even if you are never a great player, you will always be able to play the game a bit with friends and maybe even teach it to your own children someday."

"I think I see what you are saying," said Todd. "When you do something, it changes you."

"Exactly!" Mr. Peabody agreed. "If you play, you'll be

a player. And if you play over and over again it will work a lasting change in you that will be with you all your life. In the case of basketball, perhaps all it will mean is that someday you will shoot baskets in the driveway with your children and share your joy of the game. But some people will say that's a lot."

"It is a lot!" chirped Olivia. "I mean, my Dad does that with us and it has really helped me. Last year I couldn't even dribble. I wanted to go out for the team at school, but I was embarrassed. Dad took some time with me and Todd to play in the driveway and now I'm not embarrassed at all. I like playing in front of crowds."

"She's a big show off," said Todd. "But she's right. Dad helped us both a lot. I was embarrassed to play with friends too. I'm not the class star now and I probably never will be, but I'm comfortable on the court. In fact, I'm trying hard to practice an hour every night after school so I make the team next year. But now I realize, Mr. Peabody, that even if I don't make the team, my effort won't be wasted. I will still improve, and that will make the game more fun for me no matter what happens in life."

"You both have a lot of insight," said Mr. Peabody. He started to rise from the booth. "It's time for me to go to work. You asked me for the Secret of Wealth and I think you have it now. It's not easy, but it is simple. In fact, it's as simple as one, two, three.

"One, make it your goal to be wealthy. Two, get in touch with your abundance by sharing it, no matter how small it may seem. Become a giver — of your money, of your time, of your concern. Spare something. Share something. Three, stick to your behavior when you have doubts. Remind yourself of your goal often.

"If you do these things — stick to your giving and remind yourself often that you have more than you need —soon enough you will begin to enjoy all the deep blessings of wealth."

I've got it," said Todd. "You've given us the Secret of Wealth: Generosity Fosters Abundance."

Mr. Peabody smiled. It seemed to be a broader smile than the twins had ever seen before.

"I've got to run now," said Mr. Peabody, rising from his side of the booth. "But you have it now. You have the Secret of Wealth. I hope you don't forget it."

"We won't," said Olivia. "We will always remember."

Generosity Fosters Abundance.

Postscript

Several years ago I went to Haiti to document the destitution of its poorest people and the contributions being made by mission workers there. In the packet of materials I received before I departed was a small brochure about a school in Cite Soleil, the most dreadful part of Haiti's capital city, Port au Prince.

Cite Soleil is a place where open sewers wind their way in crooked streams down dirt paths that serve as streets, sidewalks and cemeteries.

In the school's brochure was an invitation from its founder, a Belgian priest who ran the school and provided its students with what was usually their only meal of the day. His invitation read like a pitch for a weekend at an expensive health spa. He said that the visitor would leave feeling renewed, enriched and energized.

As I read the simple brochure with its incongruous appeal, I concluded that the man either had a demented grasp of reality or that his tongue was firmly planted in his cheek.

After I visited his school I knew better.

We arrived at lunch time. Hundreds were served in less than an hour in a spirit of festival. A band played. People danced and clapped. Smiles beamed all around. Never before had I seen such a spirit in a school — indeed, in any institutional setting. It truly was a place of joy and purpose.

Despite the students' enduring destitution, they celebrated their incredible good fortune to be at this place where they were fed porridge and knowledge in equally generous portions.

In the course of my short stay in Haiti, I met many people who were materially poor to an extent I have never seen anywhere else. Many also suffered in other ways. Some were lepers, badly disfigured. Others were crippled and aged, sleeping on the floor of tiny, damp cells. Some lay helpless in beds where they would soon die. Nearly all of them were joyful and grateful for our interest in them.

I returned home a changed man — a wealthy one.

People in the poorest nation of the Western Hemisphere, people among the poorest anywhere in the world, gave me new eyes to see. They freed me from the bonds of poverty and self-pity.

How did they do this? Having seen the hard and meager circumstances of their existence, it was impossible for me to ever again take for granted the great endowment of blessings I had been given.

Not long after I returned from Haiti my wife called me in some distress. Our mechanic said we needed two new tires and our cupboards were nearly bare that month. "Can we do it?" I asked. She assured me that we could put the purchase on a credit card and pay it off over the next several months — but she was still distressed at our bad fortune.

I was in a different place. "Thank God we can handle

it," I said, feeling truly blessed. My wife was looking for sympathy, so my answer was not the most sensitive one a loving husband could offer. But it reflected my new- found perspective on things.

A morning or two later I awoke to find my children at the breakfast table fighting. In fact, their screams and taunts woke me. In the kitchen my wife was nearing the end of her wits trying to get the children to behave charitably toward one another. The squabbling had to be stopped, but even as it escalated a thought crossed my mind: "Thank God they are healthy enough to fight!"

I do not want to romanticize poverty. There is nothing romantic about the destitution that stalks the people of Haiti — or, for that matter, many other parts of our world. But I find it wonderfully ironic that these desperately poor people could make me a wealthy man and free me from worry about my material circumstances.

The Secret of Wealth is born inside you. But it grows and showers your life with great blessings only when you live its truth: Generosity fosters abundance. It really does. I guarantee it.

And I should know — because I am America's Wealthiest Man.

But I fervently believe that you can find as much abundance in your own life. Just remember the Secret — and celebrate it every day of your life.

- Owen Phelps

Acknowledgements

It is said that we should save the best for last. And so I have done that. For me this is the very best part about writing *The Secret of Wealth* — the opportunity to thank those who have helped me produce this book so that I could share some of my most closely held convictions with you.

I begin the process knowing that I will forget to mention someone to whom I am deeply indebted, and so I will hurt a person I set out to thank. Whoever you are — and I earnestly hope there is only one of you — please accept my apologies. Also feel free to call and express your sorrow, because when I hurt people I want to make amends.

Let me begin by thanking four teachers who continue to take time for me and contribute to my formation: my second grade instructor, Ann Walters, and college professors Larry Fedewa, Ray Stroik and Frank Wood.

I want to thank my colleagues who have informed and guided my thinking about the issues raised here. Among so many I must single out these: Mike Cieslak, Chris Gunty, Richard Haas, Dave Hougan, Msgr. Bob Hoffman, Bob Lockwood, Patrick Moynihan, Greg Jiede, Ed Murray, Bob Pfundstein, John Sentovich and Penny Wiegert. I most especially want to thank Wayne Lenell, who offered me invaluable guidance in preparing to be a book author and who always provides a fresh and unique perspective, and Sue Sabrowski, who has saved my professional life from chaos for many years. She was the first colleague to read this manuscript, and in doing so she saved me from some embarrassing errors while giving me the encouragement me to proceed.

I want to thank Phil Hodges and Ken Blanchard, successful book authors in their own right, for encouraging me and helping me to launch my own book writing career. Phil's favorable comments about my first book appeared on its back cover, and he offered helpful feedback about this one. Ken was kind enough to preview this manuscript and let me quote him about its merits on the back cover.

I'm grateful to several friends, acquaintances and classmates who have helped guide my thinking or provided feedback on the manuscript — or both — including: Julie (Fischer) Benedict, Chris Cable, Dennis Fertig, Gregg Franchini, John Gile, John Hartz, Greg Jiede, Dick and Nancy Kunnert, Sean Murray, Gene Maule, Tom Nichols, Gregory Pierce, and Jacque and Jim Schutz. Gregg and Julie deserve special mention for their extensive feedback, and Julie for so carefully proofreading the manuscript.

I want to thank my recent mentor, Chuck Sauber, who may be the wisest man and most enlightened business owner I have ever known, and whose observations and example were very helpful in shaping this book.

I owe a debt of gratitude to my family members, including all of my nine siblings and their spouses. One of them, Mary, has passed away. But her life modeled the wisdom in The Secret of Wealth. She was a joyful woman with a large family and simple tastes. Shortly before she died, she said that one of her regrets was that she didn't have more money, which surprised the visitors who were with her that day. As their faces registered shock at this very uncharacteristic sentiment, she finished her thought: "...so that I could give more away to those who really need it." I am not sure that the rest of us are quite so unselfish, but all of my brothers and sisters and their spouses are truly generous people, and my brother Pat was especially generous with his time in discussing this book's basic principles with me over the past few years.

My mother may be my biggest supporter. After nurturing me into adulthood, she started selling for me when I ran a group of newspapers, and she's still selling for me today. Just try to visit with her without being given an opportunity to buy one — or more — of my books. Thanks, Mom, for everything.

My wife and children do way more than I deserve, and much, much more than I could ever repay. Each shares with me unique expertise, and without their praise, criticism, encouragement, insights and proofreading, this book would be no more than a dream — and a messy one at that.

Two men played particularly key roles in developing the finished product. My always conscientious and meticulous friend Dan McCullough volunteered the last, critical proofreading, and Tim Randazzo turned over his remarkably creative eye to providing the book's design. I am especially grateful for their contributions.

To all of you ... to any and all whom I might have overlooked ... and to the many more who have contributed in ways that I am simply unaware, *Thank You!*

Tell Us Your Stories About How You Discovered The Secret of Wealth

How have you learned about the Secret of Wealth in your own life?

- Were you exposed to people who had less than you — but enjoyed more abundance?

- Has there been someone in your life who has served as a wonderful model of gratitude and generosity?

- Have you suffered a great hardship that left you with a lesson about what it really means to be wealthy and to enjoy abundance?

Whatever the details of your personal story, why not share it with us and visitors to our web site? And if you don't mind, it might even end up in another book someday that helps us continue to spread the secret of true wealth.

Drop in for a visit and find out more today at

www.SOWAbundance.net

Thank you again for your time and attention. Whether or not our trails ever cross again, we wish you a life of abundance in the days ahead.

Reflection & Discussion Questions Regarding Riches and Wealth

■ The Roman philosopher Seneca said centuries ago: "No one can be poor who has enough, nor rich who covets more." What does he mean? Do I have enough?

■ Since the mid-1950s the typical real income of an American has more than doubled. That means our buying power has more than doubled. In the meantime, what has happened to our happiness? The percentage of Americans who say they are "happy" has not increased — and the percentage of people who say they are "very happy" has actually dipped a bit. Why do you think this is so?

■ According to one study, disabled and chronically ill people report a higher sense of well-being than the population at large. Why do you think this is the case?

■ According to the results of one survey, no matter how much money we make, when we're asked how much money we would need to have to "live well," we say "twice as much as we do now." That means the person making $20,000 a year thinks they need $20,000 more to "live well," but the person making $200,000 is $200,000 short of "living well." What does that suggest about the relationship between being rich and being wealthy? What does it say about the prospects of most people being able to "live well" eventually?

For more questions — and for a special section of faith-based reflection and discussion questions — visit our website at www.SOWAbundance.net

To Dig Deeper

or to

Tell Your Own Story

■ **For more questions** and information about the relationship of wealth, abundance, generosity, gratitude, meaning and happiness...

■ **For updated information** regarding the effectiveness of individual charities before you donate...

■ **For parables and true stories** that illustrate the Secret of Wealth...

■ **To tell your own story** about experiencing the connection between generosity and abundance, or to share the story of someone you know who taught you the Secret of Wealth...

Please visit our website

www.SOWAbundance.net

Attention book clubs!
Arrange a one-on-one evening with the author

Dr. Phelps welcomes opportunities to meet by phone with members of book clubs who have read his book and are interested in discussing it with him.

He's especially eager to answer your questions and to share with you relevant research findings that point to how fostering gratitude and generosity can help you enjoy better health, more happiness and a deep sense of meaning and purposeful living.

You may also want to discuss how to avoid fraudulent solicitations or how to find opportunities in your community to share your four great endowments: time, talent, treasure and touch.

To schedule a half hour meeting with your book club, email Owen at

Here4U@SOWAbundance.net

Be sure to include your name, email address, phone number, the time zone you are in and a range of dates and times that would be ideal for your book club to meet with him.

Other good books you may want to read about generosity, abundance and related topics

The Generosity Factor: Discover the Joy of Giving Your Time, Talent and Treasure (2002) by Ken Blanchard and S. Truett Cathy.

In the Streets ... In the Suites (2003) by Joe Salvaggio and Jim Stowell.

The Paradox of Success: When Winning at Work Means Losing at Life — A Book of Renewal for Leaders (2004) by John R. O'Neil.

The Progress Paradox: How Life Gets Better While People Feel Worse (2003) by Greg Easterbrook.

Working With Purpose: Finding a Corporate Calling for You and Your Business (2004) by Jane Kise and David Stark.

For more information about any of these books or to order copies for yourself and friends, visit our web site at

www.SOWAbundance.net

Owen Phelps, Ph.D.

A highly-prized speaker

As head of the Midwest Leadership Institute and a popular author and commentator, Dr. Phelps is a highly sought-after keynote speaker on a variety of topics related to wealth, generosity, gratitude, happiness and individual, team and organizational development.

He has spoken to professional audiences all across America, always getting high marks for his clear, insightful and often humorous analysis.

To inquire about his availability and fees to speak before your group, contact

Here4U@SOWAbundance.net

To order additional copies of

The Secret of Wealth

contact:

http://www.SOWAbundance.net

or

The Durand Corporation
208 E. North St.
Durand, IL 61024

http://www.MidwestLeadershipInstitute.net

or

After Nov. 1, 2007

Contact:
ACTA Publications
5559 W. Howard St.
Skokie, IL 60077
1-800-397-2282

or

Check with your local or internet bookseller.